Enid Blyton's
First Bedtime Book

In this series
Enid Blyton's Second Bedtime Book
Enid Blyton's Third Bedtime Book
Enid Blyton's Fourth Bedtime Book

Also available for younger readers
The Boy Who Turned into an Engine
The Book of Naughty Children
A Second Book of Naughty Children
Ten-Minute Tales
Fifteen-Minute Tales
Twenty-Minute Tales
More Twenty-Minute Tales
The Land of Far-Beyond
Billy-Bob Tales
Tales of Betsy May
Eight O'Clock Tales
The Yellow Story Book
The Red Story Book
The Blue Story Book
The Green Story Book
Tricky the Goblin
The Adventures of Binkle and Flip
Mr Pink-Whistle's Party
Merry Mr Meddle
Mr Meddle's Mischief
Don't Be Silly Mr Twiddle
Adventures of the Wishing Chair
More Adventures of the Wishing Chair
Rag Tag and Bobtail
Tales from the Bible

Enid Blyton

First Bedtime Book

DRAGON
Granada Publishing

Dragon Books
Granada Publishing Limited
8 Grafton Street, London W1X 3LA

Published by Dragon Books 1984

First published by Arthur Barker Ltd, 1954

Copyright © Darrell Waters Ltd, 1954

ISBN 0 583 30662 4

Printed and bound in Great Britain by
Collins, Glasgow
Set in Times

Contents

It Happened So Quickly   7

Who?   16

The Peculiar Horse   18

Can You Do This?   25

The Animal in the Tree   26

Linda Loud-Voice   35

I Look and I Look and I Look!   42

Goofy Isn't Very Clever   44

The Owl   52

Down on the Farm   53

Riddle-Me-Ree   60

Let's Make Some Sweets   61

Just One Thing After Another!   64

A Map of Fairyland   74

Give Him a Tail!   76

Look in My Shop   82

Barker's Bone   84

The Bird's Christmas Tree   94

Oh! You Horrid Boy!   96

Quick! What Shall We Do?   107

The Day of the Party   113

IT HAPPENED SO QUICKLY

JOHN had a fine aeroplane sent to him for his birthday. It was a big one, and could fly well if John wound up the elastic underneath it as tightly as he could.

It really was a beauty. 'I shall take it to school and let all the boys see it,' he told Mother.

'Well, you may take it to school just as soon as you have written to thank Uncle Norman for it,' said Mother. 'I shan't let you till you have done that, because thank-you letters ought to be written as soon as possible.'

John didn't like writing letters. Bother! Now he would have to do it that evening, because he

JOHN DIDN'T LIKE WRITING LETTERS.

had promised the boys to take his aeroplane to
show them the very next day.

Mother reminded him again that night. 'John,
if you want to take your aeroplane to school
to-morrow, don't forget that thank-you letter.'

'I'll help you, John,' said Sue, his sister. 'I'll
tell you how to spell everything. Mother's going
out, so she won't be able to help you.'

Mother went out and left some notepaper and
an envelope behind her for the children to use.
John found his pen, and some ink, and sat down

at the table. His aeroplane was beside him, big and beautiful.

Sue put the notepaper in front of him. 'How do I begin?' said John.

'You ought to know,' said Sue. 'You're eight!'

'No, you tell me,' begged John. 'Then you shall fly my aeroplane tonight. We'll take it into the dining-room – there's plenty of room there – and you shall wind up the elastic bands and fly it.'

Sue told him how to begin. John made a terrible blot. 'You ought to begin all over again,' said Sue.

'I'm not going to,' said John. 'I've already written the address. I simply can't do it all over again.'

Well, John wrote that letter very badly indeed. He made three blots, four smudges, and his writing slanted so much that it almost went off the page at the bottom.

'It's a dreadful letter,' said Sue. 'Mother would make you write it all over again, especially as it's a thank-you letter, which ought to be very neat indeed.'

'I'm not going to write any more at all,' said John fiercely. 'It's taken me half an hour already.'

'All right,' said Sue. '*I* don't want to sit here and spell the words out for you again. Seal the letter up and write the envelope.'

John stuck up the envelope, and wrote his uncle's address on it. 'Suppose Mother wants to see what I've written in the letter?' he said. 'She

'IT'S A DREADFUL LETTER,' SAID SUE.

might, you know – just to see if I've done it nicely.'

'Yes. She might,' said Sue. 'Oh – *I* know what we'll do. We'll get the sealing-wax and seal it up. Mother wouldn't undo the sealing-wax. She'd think we were good to seal up the letter and everything!'

'Yes. That's a good idea,' said John, though he had an uncomfortable feeling that they were being rather deceitful. Still, he didn't want Mother to see how badly he had written that letter!

Sue fetched the sealing wax. 'How do we melt it to seal the envelope?' asked John.

'Don't you know? You light a match, hold it to the sealing-wax, and the flame melts it – and little drops fall on to the envelope, get hard, and seal it,' said Sue impatiently. 'I've often seen Daddy do it.'

'But – what about matches?' asked John. 'You know we're not supposed to strike them. In case we burn ourselves or set the house on fire.'

'I'LL STRIKE THE MATCH AND HOLD IT UP TO THE WAX.'

'Pooh! As if striking *one* match for the sea-ling-wax would matter!' said Sue. 'I don't expect Mother would even *think* about it!'

Sue got the match-box from the mantelpiece and then the red sealing-wax from Daddy's desk. She came to the table with them. 'Now you hold the stick of sealing-wax just over the envelope, where it's stuck up,' she said. 'And I'll strike the match and hold it up to the wax. Ready?'

She struck the match and held it to the wax, but she put it too close to John's fingers. He felt the flame burning him and gave a scream. He smacked the match out of Sue's fingers. 'You bad girl! You burnt me!'

And then suddenly things happened very quickly indeed. The burning match fell on John's aeroplane, and the flimsy wings and body flared up at once. Big flames rose up, and the children screamed. Sue pushed the burning plane off the table.

It fell to the floor, where the children had left their books. The flames caught them, and the books began to burn too. The flames from the books caught Mother's arm-chair and, to the children's horror, that began to burn as well.

'Quick! Quick! Tell Cook!' screamed Sue, and the two children raced out to the kitchen. 'Cook! The house is on fire! Oh, get the fire-engine, quick!'

Cook rushed into the sitting-room. She saw the flames. Soon pails of water were being flung over the burning room, and in a few minutes the

SUE PUSHED THE BURNING PLANE OFF THE TABLE.

fire was out – just as Mother came back from seeing Granny!

She was met by two weeping, frightened children. She looked at the burnt, spoilt, wet room in surprise and dismay, and listened to Sue's sobbed-out story.

'Oh, Mother! We didn't mean to. It all happened so quickly – it was only just *one* match!'

'Yes. That's why mothers say children must never use matches till they are old enough,' said Mother. 'Just one match – and then things happen so quickly that sometimes they can't be

JOHN WEPT BITTERLY.

stopped! Oh, John – my chair – and your books – and your lovely aeroplane. All gone!'

John wept bitterly. 'Mother, I wrote my thank-you letter so badly, and we sealed it with wax so that you wouldn't undo it and see it – and it was the match we used for that, that began the fire.'

'One bad thing, however little it is, always leads to another one – which is sometimes very big!' said Mother. ' One badly-written letter – one little match – one big fire – and a lot of unhappiness! Oh, John, do remember this, dear, and you, too, Sue.'

And, after all, John had to write the letter again, because that was burnt, too. Wasn't it a dreadful thing to happen to him – and all in a moment, too!

who?

Who sat in a corner?
  Who climbed up a hill?
Who sang for his supper?
Who couldn't keep still?
Who ran from a spider?
Who lost all her sheep?
Who looked in a cupboard?
Who fell fast asleep?

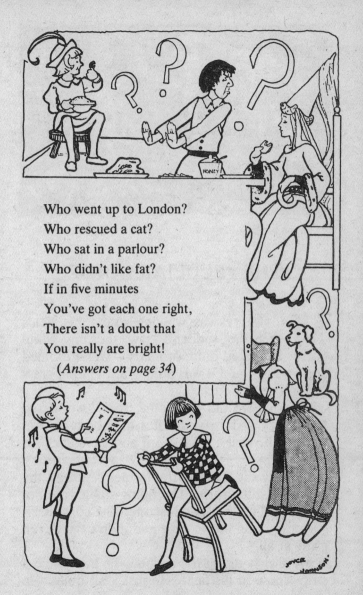

Who went up to London?
Who rescued a cat?
Who sat in a parlour?
Who didn't like fat?
If in five minutes
You've got each one right,
There isn't a doubt that
You really are bright!

(Answers on page 34)

THE PECULIAR HORSE

M R TWISTY was walking round his fields when he suddenly saw the big white horse. It looked quite ordinary – well-groomed and strong – and it was pulling at the long grass in Mr Twisty's ditch.

'Now where did *you* come from?' wondered Mr Twisty. 'All by yourself with nobody to own you. Well, well – we'll see if anyone comes for you.'

Nobody did. No nearby farmer reported the loss of a white horse. The riding-stables did not complain that they had lost one. The horse itself stayed quietly in the field and didn't try to run away at all.

Mr Twisty didn't tell anybody he had found a stray horse in his field. He just kept quiet. He should have reported it to the police, of course, but no – Mr Twisty wasn't going to do that. If anyone claimed the horse, let him come along. Mr Twisty wasn't going to bother to find the owner!

When three weeks had gone by Mr Twisty began to think of the horse as his own.

'You'll do nicely to take the cart to market for me,' he told the horse. 'You're big and strong and young. You'll work well for me.'

So the next market day Mr Twisty put the horse into the shafts of the cart, piled it high with cabbages to sell, and off he went down the lane to the market.

'If people say to me, "Hallo, Twisty, got a new horse?" I shall say, "Yes, I went over to Willham Fair and bought him there,"' said Mr Twisty. 'Then nobody will know I've kept a stray.'

Now, when Mr Twisty got to market, the horse seemed perfectly all right. Mr Twisty sat at the front of the cart with his whip, talking to his friends.

'You've got a new horse, I see,' said one of them.

'Yes – bought him over at Willham Fair some weeks back,' said Twisty.

'Nice horse,' said another man. 'Funny you haven't brought him to market before, Twisty. Willham Fair is six weeks ago now!'

'Oh, he was useful on the farm,' said Twisty.

Just then a noise came up the street and into the square. Boom-diddy-boom, boom, boom!

MR TWISTY WAS QUITE PLEASED.

It was a drum being beaten, because a band was coming to the market to play, as it often did on market day.

The horse pricked up its ears. It began to mark time to the music of the drum with its front foot – thud, thuddy-thud, thuddy-thud!

'Look at that now!' said a man, in amazement. 'That horse of yours is marking time to the music of the drum, Mr Twisty.'

Mr Twisty was quite pleased that the horse was doing such a clever thing. Thud, thuddy-thud, thuddy-thud, went the horse with its hoof, and pricked up its ears in a pleased way as the drum drew nearer.

The bandsmen came into the market square and struck up a merry tune as they marched in.

Tan-tan-tara, diddy-boom, boom, boom, fiddle-fiddle-fiddle, tirry-roola-lay!

The horse began to trot gracefully round the market square in time to the music, stepping high. It dragged the cart behind it, of course, but it didn't seem to mind that. Mr Twisty tugged at the reins and shouted, but the horse took no notice at all.

It trotted up and down whilst the music played, its head held high, and when the band stopped and only the drum sounded, the horse stopped, too, and began to mark time again with its hoof.

By this time, of course, a crowd had collected. 'Oooh! Look at that horse!' said the children to

THE BANDSMEN STRUCK UP A MERRY TUNE.

21

one another. 'Isn't it grand! Look at him marking time! Just like we do at school, but he only uses one foot and we use two.'

The band struck up again – this time a slow and dreamy waltz tune. The horse listened for a moment or two and then was off again round the market with the cart behind it. And this time it went gracefully round and round, as if it was dancing the waltz! Round and round went the cart, too, with Mr Twisty in it, feeling giddier and giddier! He slashed at the horse with the whip, but it had got the music in its ears, and nothing would stop it waltzing round and round!

'What a peculiar horse!' said the children. 'It ought to be in a circus!'

THE HORSE WENT ON DANCING ALL BY HIMSELF.

Mr Hearty, the policeman, came up, frowning. 'What's all this performance, Mr Twisty?' he said sternly. 'I shall arrest you for collecting a crowd and obstructing traffic. Stop showing off!'

Mr Twisty was scared. He leapt off the cart whilst it was still moving, and ran to the horse's head. He managed somehow to get him out of the shafts, free of the cart.

The horse went on dancing all by himself, going round and round very gracefully, stepping daintily, and sometimes turning himself round and going the other way.

'That's a circus horse, that is!' called out a small boy. 'I saw a horse like that in a circus over at Tottington three weeks ago, when I was staying with my auntie.'

'Yes – it must be a circus horse!' said the grown-ups, and they nodded their heads wisely. 'That's right.'

'Where did you say you got this horse?' asked the policeman, getting out his notebook.

'Er – er – I bought him at Willham Fair,' stammered Mr Twisty. The policeman flicked over a few pages of his notebook.

'I've got a report here of a horse straying from Mr Galliano's Circus,' he said. 'Big white horse, used to circus life, able to dance to music. But he was lost only three weeks ago, Mr Twisty. How do you explain your statement that you bought him *six* weeks ago at Willham Fair? He was in the circus then, over at Tottington.'

Mr Twisty couldn't explain at all, of course, and everyone began to jeer and call out:

'He strayed in your field and you kept him!'

'Go on, tell the truth!'

'Twisty by name and twisty by nature – that's you all right, Mr Twisty!'

'I'm afraid you'll have to come along with me,' said the policeman. Somebody caught the horse and put it back into the shafts of the cart again. The band had now stopped, so the horse was no longer dancing away on its own.

Mr Twisty had to take the horse all the way back to the circus himself. He was fined five pounds. He was jeered at by every child in the market when next he arrived.

'Well, that's the last time I keep a stray horse!' he said to himself. 'But how was *I* to know it was a circus horse? Funny business that was, the cart and the horse and me all going round in circles.'

It was – and I wish I'd been there to see it!

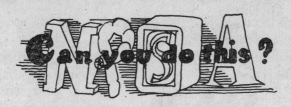

Now I'm going to make you think!
Take the letter N from Ink,
Then the letter P from Rope,
And the letter S from Soap,
Now take letter A from Play,
And write them down – N, P, S, A.
With these letters you can spell –
First a game that you know well,
Then some things that Mother takes
When she fries an egg, or bakes,
Last you'll find a little word
That for 'sleeps' is sometimes heard.

Write them down and let me see
Just how clever you can be!

(*Answers on page 51*)

The ANIMAL in the TREE

ONE day Bimbo the monkey grinned to himself and thought he'd have a little joke. So he took a round mirror from the house and fixed it neatly in a tree, whose leaves waved round it and quite hid the frame from sight.

Then Bimbo went to Billy the goat and called to him.

'Hie, Billy! Come and look in this tree. I believe your cousin's up there, hiding!'

Billy ran to the tree and looked up. He saw his own face in the mirror and he was most astonished to see what he thought was another goat up there.

'I've never heard of a goat climbing a tree before!' he said to Bimbo. 'What an extraordinary thing!'

Bimbo grinned and went running off to Buttercup the cow.

'Hie, Buttercup!' he called. 'Come and look in this tree. I believe your sister is up there!'

'Don't talk nonsense!' said Buttercup. 'No cow can climb a tree! I never heard of anything so silly!'

'I tell you, you'll see a cow up there!' said Bimbo. So Buttercup came to see. She looked up in the tree and was most surprised to see a cow's face looking down at her from among the leaves.

'Moooooo!' she bellowed. 'Look at that now! A cow in a tree! Who would have thought of that? I must go and tell the farm-yard!'

Bimbo chuckled to himself, and bounded off to Rover the dog, who was snoozing in the sunshine.

'Rover! Rover! Hie, Rover! Come and look in this tree!' chattered Bimbo. 'You'll see a dog there!'

'Dog's don't climb trees,' said Rover. 'Go and tell that tale to the cook! You'll get what you deserve then – a smack on the nose, you silly little monkey!'

'No, really, Rover, you'll see another dog there!' said Bimbo. 'He's not so nice-looking as you – but he's a fine dog. I don't know what he's doing on our farm – maybe waiting to steal your dinner!'

That was too much for Rover! He growled and got up at once. He ran to the tree and looked up. Sure enough, looking down at him was a dog! Rover sniffed – but the dog seemed to have no smell. He growled, and bared his teeth. The other dog bared his too, but Rover could not hear him growl. He jumped up and tried to reach the dog, but he couldn't.

SURE ENOUGH, LOOKING DOWN AT HIM WAS A DOG!

'Grrrrr!' said Rover, and ran off to see if his plate of dinner was safe.

Bimbo was rolling on the ground, laughing. He looked round to see whom to trick next. He saw Sally, the great fat pig, moving heavily in her sty, and he called out to her.

'Hie, Sally! Come out a minute, and look in this tree! There's a great fat pig there!'

'Don't be so silly!' said Sally. 'It will be a month of Sundays before I believe a pig can climb a tree!'

'You don't need to wait so long as that!' said Bimbo. 'Come now, and you'll see one up there all right!'

Sally grunted, and ran heavily out of her sty. When she came to the tree she lifted up her head and looked. Her small eyes nearly dropped out in astonishment when she saw a pig's face looking down at her!

'Oh, the ugly creature!' she cried. 'How did she get up there? To hide her ugly snout away, I've no doubt. Fancy a pig climbing a tree! Well, well, well! I'll just go and tell Billy the goat!'

She ran off to Billy, and as soon as they met they began to shout to one another.

'There's a goat up in that tree!' cried Billy.

'There's a pig up in that tree!' cried Sally.

Just then Buttercup ambled up, and she shook her head when she heard what they said.

'No, no!' she said. 'I've just looked. It's a cow – though goodness knows how she got up there!'

'You're all wrong,' said Rover, the farm dog. 'I've looked myself – and it's a dog. One rather

'HIE, SALLY! COME OUT A MINUTE, AND LOOK IN THIS
TREE!'

like myself, but not so good-looking. My word, I
growled at him, and showed my teeth – and the
poor creature was so scared that he couldn't
even growl back!'

'I tell you it is a goat!' said Billy.

'And I tell you it's a cow!' said Buttercup.

'A pig, pig, pig!' squealed Sally.

'Stop your pig-pig-pigging!' said Rover. 'Didn't I just say it was a dog? You're all mad! Don't you know a dog when you see one?'

'And don't you know a cow when you see one?' bellowed Buttercup indignantly.

'I distinctly saw a goat,' said Billy, 'and what is more, it wagged its beard at me! Does a pig have a beard – or a cow, or a dog?'

'WELL, THE ANIMAL I SAW HAD A SNOUT LIKE MINE,'
SAID SALLY THE PIG.

'Well, the animal *I* saw had a snout like mine,' said Sally the pig, getting crosser and crosser. 'Yes, and it grunted, I'm sure it did! Does a cow grunt – or a goat, or a dog?'

'Let's go and ask Bimbo the monkey what animal is up there,' said Rover impatiently. 'He certainly told *me* it was a dog!'

'Pardon me, he said it was a cow!' said Buttercup.

'No, a goat!' said Billy.

'A pig, pig, pig!' said Sally, squealing.

'*Will* you stop your pig-pig-pigging!' cried Rover, who couldn't bear Sally. 'Come on. Let's ask Bimbo. Where is he?'

BIMBO HAD CAREFULLY TAKEN DOWN THE MIRROR.

'I *DID* SEE A COW!' SAID BUTTERCUP.

Bimbo was nowhere to be seen. He had gone to the tree and had carefully taken down the mirror and hidden it away. When he saw the animals looking for him he hopped down the tree and went to meet them.

'Bimbo, it was a dog up that tree, wasn't it?' cried Rover.

'No, a pig, pig, pig!' squealed Sally.

'No, a cow!' mooed Buttercup.

'A goat, I tell you!' cried Billy.

'One at a time, one at a time!' said Bimbo, grinning all over his wicked monkey face. 'You saw a dog, Rover – you saw a cow, Buttercup – you a pig, pig, pig, Sally – and you a goat, Billy. Well, all I can say is that all four animals must have been up there, that's all!'

The five creatures looked solemnly up in the tree.

'There's nothing there!' said Sally.

'Not a thing!' said Rover.

'Where's the goat gone?' said Billy.

'I *did* see a cow!' said Buttercup.

'Well,' said Bimbo, 'either they were all there – or not one was there! Choose which you like, friends! It doesn't matter to me – I've had my little joke, and much enjoyed it. Good-bye!'

He went off, squealing with laughter, and the four animals looked at one another in surprise.

'Whatever did he mean?' said Rover.

And none of them knows to this day! But whenever they pass the tree, each one looks up, hoping to see a cow – or a pig – or a goat – or a dog! But I don't expect they will. Do you?

ANSWERS TO WHO?

Jack Horner; Jack and Jill; Tommy Tucker; Fidgety Phil; Little Miss Muffet; Little Bopeep; Old Mother Hubbard; Little Boy Blue; Pussy Cat; Little Johnny Stout; The Queen; Jack Sprat.

LINDA
LOUD-VOICE

THERE was once a little girl called Linda, who had a very loud and unpleasant voice. All the neighbours sighed when she went out to play in her garden because they knew there would be no peace at all. Linda would shout and yell and cry, and make all the other children as noisy as herself.

'She's rude to her mother, too,' said the neighbours. 'You can hear her shouting at her when she's told to come in for dinner. And my, you should hear her when she's put to bed at night! You might think there would be some peace for us then – but no, Linda goes on singing and yelling at the top of her voice till long after ten o'clock. Her mother can't do anything with her.'

Now, there was a little boy next door to Linda called Jeffrey. When Linda wanted to play with him she would go to the fence and shout for him. 'JEFF-REY! JEFF-REY! JEFF-REY!' she would yell, at least twenty times. She woke up all the babies asleep in their prams, and made everyone put their hands over their ears.

One day she went to the fence and yelled as usual: 'JEFF-REY! JEFF-REY!' at the top of her loud and unpleasant voice.

And what a shock she got! From under the nearby hedge a cross-looking little man got up and came over to her. 'What are you calling me for?' he said. 'What a voice you've got!'

A CROSS-LOOKING LITTLE MAN CAME OVER TO HER.

'I'm not calling *you*,' said Linda, in her usual rude way. 'I'm calling my friend next door.'

'Well,' said the little old man. 'I'm very deaf – so deaf that when my wife calls me in to dinner, I don't hear, and I have to go without my dinner. But I can hear *you* all right. I should think even the people in the next town could hear you.'

'Go away,' said Linda, who didn't like the old man at all, especially as he looked so very cross.

'I'm going,' said the old man. 'But I'm going to take you with me! You shall call me in to dinner every day, then I shan't miss it, as I so often do. I'll give you to my wife and she can tell you when to call me.'

And before Linda knew what was happening she was popped into a big sack, put over the old man's shoulder, and carried off. How she yelled!

But as everyone was quite used to hearing her yell, nobody took any notice at all. The old fellow carried her through a wood and up a lane and across a field. Then he dumped the yelling Linda down on his own doorstep.

His wife came running to the door. 'Whatever have you got in that bag?' she asked loudly. 'What a terrible noise! Is it a thunderstorm or something?'

'No. A rather rude and noisy little girl called Linda,' said the old man, with a grin. 'I was asleep under a hedge near her house, and she came out and called "JEFF-REY!" so loudly that she woke me up – and you know how very,

'WHATEVER HAVE YOU GOT IN THAT BAG?' SHE ASKED
LOUDLY.

very deaf I am. Well, of course, I thought she
was calling *me*! And I thought what a good idea
it would be if I brought her home to you,
because then when you wanted to call me in for
my dinner you could send her out to yell – and
wherever I am, I shall be sure to hear her!'

He emptied Linda out on to the kitchen floor.
She at once began to yell for her mother.

'What a voice!' said the old woman. 'I never
heard anything like it in my life. Why doesn't

her mother stop her, I wonder? Yes, I'll certainly use her to call you in to your meals, Jeffrey. And I'll use her to call the dog back when he wanders, and to shout to the cows at milking-time, and get the hens in for me when I want them. Ah, yes – she'll be very, very useful.'

'I'll run away,' screeched Linda.

'No, you won't,' said the old man, and he tied her to a post. 'Now – I'm going down to the very bottom of my long garden, Linda. Yell "JEFFREY!" and see if I can hear you.'

THE OLD MAN TIED HER TO A POST.

When he had got to the bottom of the garden, the old woman nudged Linda. 'Shout,' she said. 'Go on, shout.'

But Linda wouldn't. Then the old woman looked so angry that Linda, afraid of being smacked, opened her mouth and yelled 'JEFF-REY!'

'What a voice!' said the old woman. 'Terrible! What are your parents thinking of to let you have a voice like that? But you certainly will be very useful to me.'

Linda was frightened. She opened her mouth to yell and scream, but then she shut it quickly – that was just what this odd couple wanted her for – yelling and shouting and screaming. She had better not do it any more.

So, the next time the old lady wanted her to shout, she called so softly that the old man didn't hear her. And when she had to call the cows home, they didn't even turn their heads, her voice was so soft.

'I don't think you're going to be any use after all,' said the old lady sadly. 'Your voice seems to have gone soft. You'd better go home.'

She untied Linda from the post. 'You go back to your mother,' she said, 'and practise shouting loudly every day. I'll send Jeffrey, my old man, along each morning to hear you – and he'll bring you along as soon as your voice gets loud again. You've only got to yell "JEFF-REY! JEFF-REY!" and he'll know.'

Linda raced home as fast as her legs would take her. She went indoors very quietly. She

'I DON'T THINK YOU'RE GOING TO BE ANY USE,' SAID THE OLD LADY.

didn't slam the door. She didn't even yell for her mother.

Her mother heard her come in. 'Linda!' she called. 'Go and shout for Jeffrey and see if he will play with you.'

But Linda didn't. No – she didn't think she'd be noisy again! If she called Jeffrey, that old man might pop up his head from somewhere. So she's much quieter now, and everyone wonders why! It's such a queer story that I thought I really must tell it to you.

I Look and I Look and I Look!

Old Mister Brown
Has a very nice shop,
And outside the windows each morning
I stop,
And I look and I look and I look!
There are soldiers and motor-cars,
Teddies and trains,
Gollies and garages,
Fine aeroplanes.
Dolls that can walk,
And dolls that can talk.
A clown that goes head-over-heels,
Tunnels and rails
And monkeys with tails,
And a nice little donkey on wheels.

It's no wonder I look and I look!
It's simply no wonder I look!

GOOFY ISN'T VERY CLEVER

'Now Goofy, if you lose your handkerchief again I shall spank you,' his mother said crossly. 'It's only Wednesday – and you've lost four hankies already this week.'

'Sorry, Ma,' said Goofy.

'It's no good being sorry if you keep *on* doing the same thing,' said his mother. 'If you're *really* sorry you won't lose a single hanky again this week!'

'Ma, I won't,' said Goofy earnestly. 'I really won't, Ma. If I do you can spank me, and take

44

all the money out of my money-box to buy new hankies, and you can send me to bed with nothing to eat but bread. There now – surely that will make you believe I'm really sorry and I mean what I say about not losing any more hankies!'

His mother looked at him. 'All right, I believe you, Goofy,' she said. 'But that's a dreadful lot of punishments you're laying up for yourself! You'd better be very, very careful. Look at your hanky *now*!'

Goofy looked. It was hanging half out of his pocket, just ready to drop. He stuffed it back, but changed his mind and pulled it right out.

'I'm going to *pin* it on me, Ma,' he said. 'Then I can't possibly lose it.'

'Well, here's my very biggest safety-pin,' said Ma, and she gave Goofy an enormous one. 'Now, let me see you pin your hanky on your front.'

Goofy solemnly pinned it there. He smacked himself on the chest.

'*Now* I'm safe! The hanky can't possibly be lost, so don't worry any more, Ma!' He went off to get the basket to do the shopping.

His mother called after him: 'Goofy! Don't forget to put your sun-hat on, now – the sun is blazing down to-day, and you'll get sunstroke again if you go without your hat.'

'Right, Ma!' called Goofy, and went to the cupboard for the shopping basket. He came out with it, and carefully put the shopping-list in the bottom of the basket. Oh, Goofy was going to

SHE GAVE GOOFY AN ENORMOUS PIN.

be very, very careful about everything now! He'd show Ma he could be trusted.

He went off down the street. He quite forgot to fetch his sun-hat before he started out! The sun blazed down, tremendously hot. Goofy toiled along, panting.

He met Dame Slow. She called out to him.

'Goofy! What's your mother thinking of to send you out without your sun-hat? You'll get sunstroke again as sure as eggs are eggs!'

Goofy put his hand up to his head. His hair was burning hot! Goodness gracious, he'd forgotten his sun-hat after all! Now he would get sunstroke and feel sick again, and have a dreadful headache!

'I *can't* go all the way home again to fetch my hat,' groaned Goofy. 'What can I do?' Then he thought of a splendid idea. 'Of course! I'll knot my big hanky at the corners and wear it like a cap! Then I'll be quite all right.'

He unpinned the big safety-pin, and took his hanky off his chest. He carefully pinned the

HE MET DAME SLOW.

safety-pin back again, so as not to lose it. Then he knotted his hanky at the corners, and made a very nice little cap of it.

He slipped it over his hot head. Ah – that was better. Now he'd be all right! He went off happily to the shops, feeling very, very clever.

He did all the shopping quite well. Then he set off home again, thinking how pleased his

HE DID ALL THE SHOPPING QUITE WELL.

mother would be with him. She might even give him a slice of the new fruit cake!

Now just as he was going in at the front gate he sneezed.

Whooooosh-oo! He felt for his hanky at once – but, dear me, it wasn't on his chest. Goofy stared down at himself in dismay.

'Now I've gone and lost my hanky again!' he groaned. 'How *could* it have gone? The big safety-pin is still there on my chest – but the hanky isn't. It isn't in my pockets, either. Oh dear, oh dear, it's gone!'

His mother was out. Goofy felt very, very sad. He remembered the punishment he had told his mother she could give him if he lost his hanky again.

He put the shopping on the table. He went to the larder and cut himself two slices of dry bread. He took his money-box and emptied it out on the kitchen-table and wrote a little ticket beside it. 'To buy a new hanky.'

Then he climbed slowly upstairs, undressed himself, and put himself to bed.

His mother was most astonished to see him there, with the dry bread beside him, when she came home.

'Oh, Ma!' wept Goofy, 'I lost that hanky, I did, I did! Though it was *pinned* on me, too! So I've emptied my money-box, and got myself some dry bread, and put myself to bed. Now you've got to spank me.'

'But, Goofy,' said his mother, puzzled, 'what's that on your head?'

49

GOOFY PUT UP HIS HAND TO HIS HEAD.

Goofy put up his hand to his head. He had *quite* forgotten that he had made himself a sun-hat out of his hanky! He pulled it off, and looked at it joyfully, very red in the face.

'Oh, Ma! I *didn't* lose it! I can get up! I can have my money back! I just made a sun-hat of my hanky and then forgot all about it! Ma, I've been very, very silly.'

'I could have told you that long ago,' said his

mother, laughing. 'Get up quickly, Goofy – there's the biggest slice of fruit cake that ever you saw waiting on the kitchen-table for you!'

Well, well, well – some people do peculiar things, don't they?

ANSWERS TO CAN YOU DO THIS?
The letters N, P, S, A when re-arranged, will make a game, SNAP – something that Mother uses, PANS – and another word for sleeps, which is NAPS.

51

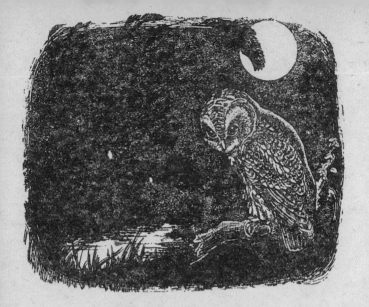

THE OWL

Who is it flying at dark of night,
Who is it giving the mice a fright,
Calling mournfully all night through,
Hoo-hoo-HOO,
Hoo-hoo-HOO!

Here on shadowy wings I go
Looking for mice in the fields below,
And they cry 'Who is it, oh who are YOU?'
And they run when they hear my
Hoo-hoo-HOO!

Down on the Farm

THE farmer's wife was very angry indeed. She came running up to Simon and Jenny, her face very red and cross.

'You bad children! You've left that field-gate open and the cows are getting out. Tiresome little things you are, never thinking of what may happen if you leave gates open! You want a good spanking!'

Jenny was frightened and couldn't say a word. But Simon spoke up quickly.

'We haven't been into the field. We didn't leave any gate open. If we ever open a gate we always shut it again after us.'

'It's no good telling me stories, as well as doing careless things,' scolded the farmer's wife. 'Who could have left the gate open if you didn't?'

'Well, we saw some other children going up the lane,' said Simon. 'Can I chase the cows back for you?'

'Certainly not! I won't have you frightening the poor animals, and hitting them with hard sticks, as I've no doubt you'd love to do!' said the farmer's wife. 'If ever I see you down this lane again I'll tell my dog to go and chase you away!'

'But please, we really didn't leave –' began Simon again, but the woman had gone off after the cows.

Jenny began to cry. 'Don't let's come here again,' she said.

'Don't cry,' said Simon. 'It's all right. You know we didn't even open a gate, so how could we have let the cows out? It must have been those children we met.'

They went on up the lane. Suddenly a duck came walking out of a big bush on the other side of the hedge. She looked surprised to see the children and waddled back through the hedge again.

'What is she here for?' wondered Simon. 'She's right away from the other farm-ducks. They are down by the pond. What is she doing in that bush?'

'Do you think she's got a nest?' asked Jenny.

'We'll see,' said Simon. 'We can't leave any

gates open if we crawl through this gap in the hedge!'

So they crawled through, and then pushed their way into the middle of the thick bush. A low quack-quack greeted them. The duck was there, sitting comfortably on a nest she had made!

She got up and went towards the two children – and they saw that she had twelve eggs there – and one was just hatching!

'Look – the shell is breaking – there's a dear little duckling coming out!' said Jenny.

THE DUCK WAS SITTING COMFORTABLY ON A NEST.

The children knelt there, watching. 'You know, we ought to go down to the farm and tell them about this,' said Simon. 'Twelve new ducklings – they'd be pleased to have those. If they're left here the rats might get them.'

'What! Go down to that farm again!' cried Jenny. 'I won't! Let them lose the eggs!'

'Oh, no, Jenny – think of the baby ducklings,' said Simon. 'The duck is tired of sitting now. When her babies are hatched she'll probably wander off and I'm sure the rats will get them – or a fox.'

'Oh, dear,' said Jenny. 'Well, you go, Simon. I daren't. I'll stay here.'

So Simon went, not feeling very brave. He got to the farm and out in the yard he saw the farmer's wife. She looked up, saw him, and frowned. 'Didn't I tell you –' she began.

'Please,' said Simon, 'I've just come to say that my sister and I have found a duck's nest up the lane in a bush behind the hedge – and there are twelve eggs and I think they are about to hatch.'

'Well, well – so that's where Dilly Duck went each day!' cried the farmer's wife. 'Just hatching, did you say? Well, what an exciting bit of news!'

And she hurried all the way up the lane with Simon. Jenny was horrified to see her again – and very surprised when the farmer's wife smiled at her and said, 'What a piece of luck that you found that sitting of eggs! I *am* glad! I'll take them all back with me this very minute, so that

HE GOT TO THE FARM, AND SAW THE FARMER'S WIFE.

they will hatch in the farm-yard and be safe from foxes and rats!'

She gathered them carefully into a basket. One egg had hatched out into a tiny, crumpled duckling. 'Can you carry it gently?' she asked Jenny. 'And you, boy, can you make the duck waddle slowly down the road in front of us? Well, well – what a find!'

And down the lane went the little procession, the farmer's wife with the basket, Jenny with the

DOWN THE LANE WENT THE LITTLE PROCESSION.

tiny new duckling, and Simon guiding the wad-
dling duck.

The farmer met them and laughed. His wife
told him what had happened.

'These children are very kind and sensible.
When they found the nest they didn't rob it or
spoil it, they told me about it. Good, sensible
children!'

'But you thought we were story-tellers, and
had left your gate open,' said Jenny, finding her
tongue.

'Ah, well, I know I was wrong about you
now,' said the farmer's wife. 'Children who can

58

act like you've acted over my duck and her eggs couldn't possibly leave gates open. That I do know. I'm sorry I was cross with the wrong children. Now, you come and feed my hens with me, and we'll see if there are two nice brown eggs for you to take home for your breakfast.'

Well, they fed the hens, and they found two large brown eggs in one of the nests. They were warm and smooth. The farmer's wife put them into a tiny basket with some straw.

'There you are,' she said. 'And if you come to-morrow at tea-time, my two nephews will be here, and I'll give all of you the best tea you've ever had!'

So Simon and Jenny are going back again to-morrow, and I quite expect they will make friends with the nephews and spend most of their holidays at the farm!

Riddle·Me·Ree

My first is in sailor but isn't in boat,

My second's in tailor and also in coat,

My third is in soldier but isn't in gun,

My fourth is in baker but isn't in bun;

My fifth is in jockey but isn't in speed,

My whole makes you feel very happy indeed.

Where will you find it? Well, if you look,

You'll see quite a dozen in this very book!

(Answer on page 73)

60

LET'S MAKE SOME SWEETS!

ARE you busy? Would you like to spend a little time with me this afternoon, and make yourself some sweets? Very well, then, come along!

Now, let's see – what shall we make? Do you like chocolate raisins, or chocolate nuts? I thought you did. We'll make those then. Let me look into my larder and see if I have any raisins to spare. Yes, I have a few, but not very many. You must run out into the lane and see if you can find a few hazel nuts on the hedges. We'll use those too.

Did you find some nuts? Good. We'll shell them, and put them beside the raisins. Now I must find a bar of plain chocolate. Here's one, all ready!

We shall want a sheet of grease-proof paper on the table near the nuts and raisins. We want a large saucepan of boiling water and a small earthenware mixing bowl, too.

Now we'll cut the chocolate into small pieces. You can put each piece into the bowl. Is that saucepan of water beginning to boil on the stove? Yes, it is. Hand me the bowl of cut-up bits of chocolate and I will stand it carefully inside the boiling water. I'd rather you didn't put it there yourself in case you scald your hand.

Look at the chocolate in the bowl! The heat is beginning to make it melt. Stir it with this spoon. Now it's all melted, and I will lift the saucepan on to the kitchen table.

Now comes the exciting part – you can do it all if you like! Here is a long pin for you. Jab it into a nut or a raisin, and then dip it into the melted chocolate. That's right – turn it about – and now lift it out again. It is all covered with the melted chocolate! Do you see how it hardens as soon as you lift it out of the bowl?

Put your chocolate raisin down on the grease-proof paper to dry off. Now jab another nut or raisin with your pin.

Into the melted chocolate it goes – turn it about – out it comes with a coat of chocolate – and joins our first sweet on the grease-proof paper.

There is enough melted chocolate for all our nuts and raisins. We will find a little dish for each kind of sweet. Isn't it fun to make our own?

Now off you go to your mother with your small dishes. How surprised she will be to hear you say, 'Which will you have, Mummy – a chocolate nut or a chocolate raisin? I've made them all myself!'

JUST ONE THING AFTER ANOTHER !

GEOFFREY was working alone in the class-room, after the others had gone out to play. He was finishing his map. It was a beauti-ful map, and Geoffrey was very proud of it. So was his teacher.

'It's one of the best this class has done,' he told Geoffrey. 'I shall pin it up on the wall, and it can be one of the show-things for the parents to see at half-term.'

So Geoffrey was feeling very cheerful as he worked. He was using a green crayon for the woods showing on the map, and when he had finished those, he wanted a blue one for the sea.

But his blue one wasn't there. He must have lost it on the way to school. Blow!

He looked at his teacher's desk. Mr White always kept a fine blue crayon there for marking and correcting.

'I shouldn't take anything off his desk without permission,' thought Geoffrey, 'but what does a little thing like this matter? I shan't use the blue pencil for long!'

So he took it off Mr White's desk and began to crayon the sea blue in his map.

And then the point snapped right off! Geoffrey stared at it impatiently. 'You *would* break just at this very minute!' he said. 'Now I've got to sharpen you well before I put you back, or Mr White will guess I've borrowed you.'

He hadn't got a sharpener. He knew Peter had a lovely sharp one in his desk, so he thought he would borrow that. Peter had forbidden anyone to borrow it without permission because it was such a beauty and he didn't want it spoilt.

'Well, Peter won't know,' said Geoffrey to himself. So he reached over to Peter's desk, opened it, and took out the pencil sharpener.

He went to sharpen the pencil over by the waste-paper basket. But just as he was finishing it he heard someone coming!

In a fright he put the pencil and sharpener hurriedly into a nearby pencil-box. Peter wouldn't be at all pleased if he saw he was using his pencil sharpener! He must hide it at once!

But the box wouldn't shut properly with an extra pencil and sharpener in it – they peeped out half-way!

So, just as the door opened, Geoffrey pushed the pencil-box into the pocket of his blazer! It stuck out rather, so he kept his elbow pressed down over it.

HE HEARD SOMEONE COMING!

'Still at work, Geoffrey?' said Mr White's
voice, and Geoffrey gave him a feeble smile.
'I've come to fetch you to play games for ten
minutes. Come along. We're all waiting for
you.'

So Geoffrey left his map and went with Mr
White, guiltily keeping his elbow over the pencil-box to hide it. Whose box was it? It must be
Keith's. He'd better not let Keith see it then, or
he would have plenty to say about people who
went off with his pencil-box!

'Take off your blazer,' said Mr White, as they
came by the cloakroom. 'Go and hang it up – it's
too hot to play in it to-day.'

Geoffrey went into the cloakroom. He stood there wondering what to do. 'If I hang up my blazer on its peg, the pencil-box will show, and the boys will soon spot it,' he thought. 'I'd better stick it in the cupboard where the odds and ends are kept – the old balls and bats and things. Nobody will see it there.'

So he opened the cupboard door and threw in his blazer, with the pencil-box still in the pocket. Then out he went to play.

When the game was over, the boys trooped back into school. Some went to put on their blazers and some didn't. Geoffrey didn't. He didn't want to drag it out of the old cupboard

'NOBODY WILL SEE IT THERE.'

with all the boys looking on! He could easily fetch it later on when the cloakroom was empty.

But long before that, some very awkward questions were asked.

'Anyone borrowed my blue pencil?' asked Mr White, hunting for it. Geoffrey didn't say a word!

'I say – my pencil sharpener's gone!' said an indignant voice a little later. 'Who's got it?' That was Peter speaking, of course. Still Geoffrey didn't say a word. How silly of him!

'Sir – my pencil-box has *completely* disappeared!' said another voice, a minute later. That was Keith, who simply could not imagine why his box had disappeared into thin air.

GEOFFREY BEGAN TO FEEL SCARED.

68

'Is anyone playing silly tricks?' asked Mr White. 'If anyone has taken my pencil, Peter's sharpener, and Keith's pencil-box, will they please produce them now? The joke is no longer funny.'

Geoffrey began to feel scared. Why ever hadn't he spoken up at once? It was ten times more difficult now! He began to shiver a little with fright.

Mr White noticed it. 'You're cold, Geoffrey. Fetch your blazer. Hurry up, please. Anyone else who feels cold can also get his blazer.'

Nobody else did, so Geoffrey thankfully went off to the cloakroom to get his blazer out of the cupboard.

But it wasn't there! He stared blankly at the cupboard. He had put it there, he knew he had. *Now* what was he to do? He hunted round everywhere, but he couldn't find it.

He went back to the classroom. 'Sorry sir, I can't find it,' said Geoffrey. 'It's – er – it's gone.'

'What! Something else gone!' said Mr White. 'This is beyond a joke. Who has taken Geoffrey's blazer? Did you hang it on your own peg, Geoffrey?'

'Yes, sir,' said Geoffrey, who felt that he simply *couldn't* say he had put it into the old cupboard.

Then the door opened and the Head's wife bustled in. She held a blazer in her hand! It was Geoffrey's, and from the pocket the pencil-box stuck out.

'Mr White! I'm sorry to interrupt,' she said.

THE HEAD'S WIFE HELD A BLAZER IN HER HAND!

'But I found this blazer in the old cupboard this morning. It doesn't seem to be marked with the owner's name, though it should be, of course. I think it must belong to one of your boys here.'

'It's Geoffrey's!' said John, at once. 'His has got an odd button. It's yours, isn't it, Geoff?'

Geoffrey nodded. Mr White took the blazer and handed it to Geoffrey. He looked cross. 'If anyone else throws a boy's blazer into the cupboard I shall punish him,' he said. 'It's a silly trick.'

'Sir! That's my pencil-box sticking out of the pocket!' shouted Keith suddenly. He pounced on it and took it out. 'See? Who put it there?'

70

'And look – isn't that my pencil sharpener sticking half-way out of the lid!' cried Peter. 'It *is*! How did it get there, I'd like to know!'

The box was opened wide to set it free – and the blue pencil belonging to Mr White dropped out, too. He picked it up from Keith's desk.

'The missing pencil!' he said. 'All very interesting, but extremely mysterious. Can anyone explain this mystery? I feel that one of you can. Speak up, please.'

Well, there was no help for it then. Geoffrey had to own up.

'Sir,' he began, standing up, very red in the face, 'I can explain it. I borrowed your blue

'THE MISSING PENCIL!' HE SAID.

pencil and broke it. I borrowed Peter's
sharpener. I heard someone coming and shoved
the pencil and sharpener into the nearest pencil-
box. But it wouldn't shut, and I put it into my
pocket. It showed there, sir, so I didn't like to
hang my blazer on my peg in case the others
spotted the box.'

'I see. So you had to throw your blazer into
the old cupboard to hide it,' said Mr White
sternly. 'And now I suppose you feel as if you
want to go and hide yourself somewhere, too,
don't you?'

'Yes,' said Geoffrey, in a small voice. 'I'm
sorry, sir.'

'GEOFFREY HASN'T COME OUT OF THIS VERY WELL,' SAID
MR WHITE.

'Beast, to borrow my sharpener!' said Peter.

'You might have owned up!' said Keith. 'I hunted for ages for my box.'

'Geoffrey hasn't come out of this very well,' said Mr White, putting his pencil back on his desk. 'It's a pity. I'm afraid I shan't want your map up on the wall now, Geoffrey.'

'No, sir,' said poor Geoffrey. 'You see, sir – I didn't *mean* to do all that – it was just one thing after another, sir – first the pencil, then the sharpener, then the box, then my blazer – and now all this!'

'Yes. It's best not to do the first thing really – the one that leads to all the others – isn't it?' said Mr White. 'Well, we will now drop the subject, and if anyone has anything else to say about the matter, they must say it in the playground after school.'

The boys are thinking of quite a lot to say to Geoffrey! He's sitting doing his French now, but he's not thinking much about it.

He's saying: 'If only I hadn't borrowed that pencil, if only I hadn't.'

Well, we've all said that kind of thing to ourselves at times. Haven't we?

ANSWER TO RIDDLE-ME-REE
Story

A Map of Fairyland

Here's a map of Fairyland,
Can you find the way,
And wander safely east to west
One very sunny day?
You mustn't pass a wizard's house,
Or venture near a witch,
You mustn't go through Goblin Land,
Or leap a magic ditch.
Beware of little paths that lead
To where enchanters dwell,
Don't even stop to make a wish
Beside a wishing-well!
But take the winding path that leads
Towards the End-of-Day,
It really is a lovely trip
When once you know the way!

GIVE HIM A TAIL!

THE clockwork mouse was worried about his tail. He kept looking at it with a frown.

'It's almost worn out,' he told the golly. 'I can't even move it any more. It got caught in the brick-box, and it got caught under the rocking-horse – and after the puppy had chewed it, it really got very bad indeed.'

'Your tail?' said the cowboy doll, coming up and swinging his lasso. 'Yes, it's dreadful, isn't it? Why don't you get a new one?'

'Don't be silly,' said the clockwork mouse. 'You know you can't go and buy tails. And don't lasso me, please. I hate that rope of yours! You're always sending it through the air trying to catch toys with it!'

Wheeeee! The rope with the loop at the end flew through the air and dropped neatly round the clockwork mouse's neck. He was very upset.

'There! You're always doing that. I hate your silly rope. Take it off my neck.'

The cowboy doll laughed. He really wasn't very kind. He took the rope off the mouse's neck. 'I can tell you where to find plenty of tales,' he said. 'See that magazine over there?'

'What? The one the children read?' said the mouse.

'Yes,' said the cowboy doll. 'Well, there are heaps of tales in there. I've heard the children say so. Why don't you get one out of the book and wear it?'

Well, that was very unkind of him, wasn't it, because the tales he meant were not the kind the mouse meant, and he knew it. The mouse meant tails to wear, and the doll meant tales to read. But he knew the clockwork mouse was only a baby and he was teasing him.

The mouse believed him. He went joyfully to the little magazine. 'Will the tail be inside the pages?' he asked.

'Of course,' said the cowboy doll. 'Some tales are long. Some are short. Take your choice!'

Poor little mouse! He turned over every page carefully. He hunted and he hunted for a long tail or a short one – but although there were plenty of stories in the book, he couldn't, of course, find a tail to put on the end of himself.

He got to the end of the book and then he began all over again. No tail anywhere! But the cowboy doll still said there were plenty there, and he wasn't looking properly, so he turned over the pages again and again!

HE TURNED OVER THE PAGES AGAIN AND AGAIN!

Then the golly came up to see what was happening. The poor little mouse was so tired out looking for tails he couldn't find that he had fallen fast asleep beside the magazine.

The cowboy doll laughed and told the golly. The golly was very angry. 'How can you be so unkind to the youngest, smallest toy here?' he said. 'Now, just you listen to me, cowboy – you've sent him hunting for a tail time and again in the children's magazine – now you've got to put one there for him to find. See?'

78

'But I can't,' said the cowboy doll. 'I haven't a tail. You know that.'

The other toys came up, looking angry, too. The cowboy felt afraid.

'It's true you haven't a tail,' said the bear. 'But you've got something else. You've got your rope – the lasso you're always catching us with. That would make a fine strong tail for the mouse!'

'But I can't give him my rope!' cried the

'I CAN'T GIVE HIM MY ROPE!' CRIED THE COWBOY DOLL.

79

cowboy doll, in horror. 'Why – it's part of my cowboy dress.'

'I don't care what it is,' said the golly. 'You've been unkind and you've got to make up for it. And we'll all be very glad indeed to see your rope on the clockwork mouse for a tail, instead of swinging in your hand. Now – give it to me!'

Well, there was no help for it – the cowboy had to give up his rope. The golly and the bear undid the loop at the end, and then laid the little rope carefully inside another magazine.

'Now, when the mouse wakes up, you tell him the tail you meant wasn't in that other magazine, it was in this one,' said the bear. 'Sh– he's waking now.'

The mouse opened his eyes. The cowboy spoke to him. 'Mouse – I made a mistake. The tail is in *this* book, not the other one. Just have a look and see.'

Well, of course, the mouse found the rope at once, and he didn't for one minute think it was the cowboy's rope! He really and truly thought it was a new tail!

He was full of joy. The bear took off his old worn-out one for him, and sewed on the new one. It was very long and strong.

'Oh, isn't that good! Thank you, bear,' said the mouse. 'I do feel happy now. And thank you, cowboy doll, for telling me where to find a tail!'

The cowboy doll was upset and cross – but nobody minded. 'It serves him right,' said the bear. 'He made himself a nuisance with that

THE BEAR SEWED ON THE NEW ONE.

rope – and the mouse will never lasso us with it,
I'm sure.'

He doesn't, of course. It makes a fine tail, and
he's really very proud of it indeed.

LOOK
in my
SHOP

Look in this shop, and you'll see I sell
Something beginning with letter L,
And up in a corner, tucked away,
Are things beginning with letter K.
Five useful things all begin with B,
And three here and there with the letter P,
And here is something whose middle is I,
And a dear little creature that ends in Y.

If you've found them all, I really must say
You're good at guessing a puzzle today!

(*Answers on page 112*)

BARKER'S BONE

BARKER was very pleased. He had been shopping with his mistress, and had carried the basket for her, and she had given him a fine reward:

It was the biggest bone he had ever had in his life. It was the meatiest, too. Barker carried it all the way home in his mouth, giving it a tiny little crunch now and again.

The other dogs saw him and his bone. They would have come and sniffed at it, but Barker's mistress always carried a stick, and they knew she would use it if anyone upset her precious Barker. Still, they sniffed it from far off and wondered if they could possibly get a bit of it.

Barker had a friend, another little dog called Tinks. Tinks lived next door to him, and the two often went for walks together. Sometimes Barker shared a meal with Tinks because he didn't have enough to eat. His kennel was cold, too, because he never had enough straw.

Tinks loved Barker and would do anything in the world for him. It was fine to have a friend like Barker!

'I'm lucky,' thought Tinks. 'All the other dogs would like to have Barker for their very special friend – but he's mine!'

Barker trotted in at Tinks's gate to show him his fine new bone. Tinks sniffed at it and almost licked it – but it isn't good manners for a dog to lick another dog's bone, so he didn't.

'I'll share this bone with you, Tinks,' said Barker generously. 'You look thin and hungry again. I'm going to bury it in a safe place now, but this evening I'll dig it up again and we'll take turns at chewing and biting.'

'Oh, thank you!' said Tinks joyfully. That would be something to look forward to, all day long!

Barker trotted into his own garden gate, the bone still in his mouth. He went into the back garden, right down to the rubbish-heap. He scraped away some of the rubbish and put the bone there. He covered it up carefully. There! Nobody could possibly see it!

Tinks knew where it was, of course. He knew that Barker always hid his bones in that rubbish-heap. And this time somebody else knew, too.

It was Spot, the dog who lived in the house that backed on to Barker's garden. He happened to be at the bottom of his garden, when Barker came down to the rubbish-heap to bury his bone.

Spot looked through a hole in the fencing.

SPOT LOOKED THROUGH A HOLE IN THE FENCING.

My, what a bone! Surely it was the biggest any
dog had ever had! Spot's mouth watered as he
watched Barker bury it in the rubbish-heap.

That afternoon Spot went to tell the other
dogs of the district about the wonderful bone.
He gathered them all round him – Buster,
Mouser, Whiskers, Bonzo, Lassie, and Tinks.
He told them about the bone.

'I vote we go and dig it up and share it among
ourselves,' said Spot. 'A big bone like that
ought not to go to one dog.'

'But he's *earned* it,' said Lassie. 'He carries

86

his mistress's basket every day for her. It is his wages, really. It's his own bone.'

'Oh, well, you needn't come if you don't want to,' said Spot. 'What about it, you others?'

'You're not to go and take Barker's bone,' said Tinks fiercely. 'It's his! It would be stealing, if you go and take it. I won't let you.'

'Shall we all bite Tinks?' asked Spot, and all but Lassie snarled and showed their teeth.

Tinks fled. He knew quite well he could not fight so many dogs. He went to find Barker. But

'YOU'RE NOT TO GO AND TAKE BARKER'S BONE,' SAID
TINKS FIERCELY.

Barker had gone out with his mistress till the evening. What was he to do?

'I know! I'll go into his garden, dig up the bone before the other dogs get it, and bury it in my *own* garden!' said Tinks. 'I'll bury it near the sitting-room window. No dog would dare to come and find it there.'

So that's what he did. He found the bone in the rubbish-heap, ran back to his own garden and buried it in the bed just under the sitting-room window. There! Now he could wait till Barker came back, and could give him his bone in safety.

But Spot saw Tinks digging up the bone and running off with it. He danced with fury the other side of the fence. He rushed straight off to tell the others.

And when Barker came home that night and found that his bone was gone, the dogs came and told him who had taken it.

'It was Tinks,' they said. 'Spot saw him. Tinks, your best friend! Pooh, we always thought he wasn't worth much. Now you've lost your bone.'

'I don't believe it,' said Barker.

'Well, you go and look in the bed under the sitting-room window next door,' said Spot. 'It's there! Tinks put it there.'

Barker ran off, puzzled and sad. Surely, surely Tinks, his friend, wouldn't have stolen his bone and hidden it to eat by himself!

He dug in the bed – and there was his big bone, carefully buried. Barker ran off with it.

'IT WAS TINKS,' THEY SAID. 'SPOT SAW HIM.'

To think that Tinks, his friend, had taken it! Oh, what a wicked dog he must be!

'I shall fight him,' said Barker. 'I shall bite his ears. I shall teach him not to steal my bones, and pretend to be my friend!'

So when he met Tinks coming home from a walk he flew at him. He snapped at his ears and bit a piece off the tip of one. He bit Tinks in the leg. He growled and snarled as if he were fifty dogs rolled into one.

Tinks fled. What was the matter with Barker? Oh dear, oh dear, his friend had fought him and

TINKS FLEW AT HIM.

bitten him! Tinks curled up on a mat in the shed, very unhappy indeed.

He thought of Barker's bone. He must take it back to him. Perhaps Barker would tell him why he was so very angry.

So he went to dig up the bone. But it was gone, of course. Barker had it now, and was at that very moment crunching it up in his kennel. He was still angry – but oh, how nice the bone was!

Tinks was terribly upset to find that the bone had gone. Could those other dogs have dared to come and take it, after all? Well, if so, he must certainly tell Barker.

Very much afraid, Tinks padded softly into the next-door garden. Barker heard his feet coming and growled. He pushed his bone under the straw of his kennel and sat up to see who was coming.

'Barker! It's me, Tinks!' said Tinks. 'Please don't fight me again. I've come to tell you something.'

'I know what you've come to tell me,' said Barker angrily. 'You've come to tell me you stole my bone. Well, I know it. All the other dogs told me how they saw you digging it out of the rubbish-heap and running off with it. Mean thing!'

Tinks trotted right round to the entrance of the big kennel. He was sad and angry.

'Barker! Did you believe that? It's true I dug up your bone – but only because I heard the other dogs planning to steal it. You ask Lassie! She was like me, she didn't want to steal it.'

'Well – what happened?' said Barker.

'I thought I'd better go and get it and hide it away for you, till you came home,' said Tinks. 'That's all. But I couldn't give it to you because you flew at me and fought me. And now, oh Barker – the bone's gone! I looked for it where I put it – in the bed under the sitting-room window – and it's gone! The other dogs must have come to get it after all.'

Barker sat still for quite a long while and said nothing. He was feeling upset and ashamed. Tinks hadn't stolen his bone – he had taken it to keep it safe for him! And he, Barker, had flown

TINKS WAS SAD AND ANGRY.

at him and bitten him and called him names.
Why hadn't he trusted poor Tinks? He might
have known he wouldn't steal a bone!

'Tinks. Come into my kennel,' he said. 'Let
me lick where I bit you. Come along. And look,
take my bone. I don't want any more of it. Chew
off the meat and crunch it up. Go on!'

Tinks was most astonished. He came timidly
into the kennel, and Barker began to lick the
places where he had bitten him. Tinks smelt the
bone. He gave it a lick. He gave it a little nibble.
He was hungry and the bone was very good!

'I thought you'd *stolen* my bone,' said Barker
sadly. 'Please forgive me, Tinks. The other dogs
said they had seen you stealing it, and I didn't

stop to find out if it was true. I just flew at you.'

'Oh, was that all?' said Tinks. 'Well, that doesn't matter a bit. I don't need to forgive you. You're my friend, so there's nothing to forgive. It was just a mistake.'

And he licked Barker lovingly. They were friends again. Yes, better friends than ever!

You should see the bones and tit-bits that Barker brings Tinks now. You should see him share his kennel with Tinks when the nights are very cold. You should see how he sticks up for him if any of the others go for Tinks!

'It must be good to have a friend like that,' the other dogs say. 'Tinks doesn't deserve it!'

But *I* think he does. Don't you?

The Bird's Christmas Tree

I've bought a little Christmas tree,
I've dressed it top to toe,
It's on the garden-table – see,
Isn't it a show!

You won't see any candles there,
Or ornaments or toys,
No fairy doll with fluffy hair–
It's not for girls and boys!

I've dressed the tree with other things,
With bacon rind and bread,
And peanuts hanging down in strings,
And spray of berries red.

Blackbird, starling, robin, jay,
Fly down and see your tree,
I've put it there for Christmas Day,
A little gift from me!

Oh! You horrid boy

'WILL you go to old Mrs Ronaldson's for me, and ask her if she can possibly come and help with the washing on Monday?' said Mother to Richard.

Richard was busy with a big jigsaw puzzle. 'Oh, dear,' he said. 'Must I go now, this very minute?'

'*I'll* go if you're too busy with your puzzle,' said Sally, his sister. 'I'd like to go through the woods. The leaves are turning such lovely colours now.'

But Mother didn't like Sally to go walking alone in the woods. Richard looked up at once when Sally spoke.

'No, I'll go,' he said. 'Daddy said you mustn't go in the woods without me, you know that. I can finish the jigsaw when I come back.'

'That's nice of you, Richard,' said Mother. 'Sally, you go, too, if you want the walk.'

'Right,' said Sally, and the two of them went to get their hats and coats. They set off down the lane and then turned into the wood. It was a bright, sunny day in early autumn, and the trees were beginning to change colour. Sally skipped along with Richard behind her.

They went through the wood and at last came to a stile. Over it they climbed and went up the little hill to Mrs Ronaldson's cottage. They knocked on the door.

Nobody came to open it. They knocked again, and Sally called loudly: 'Mrs Ronaldson! It's us, Richard and Sally.'

Still there was no answer. Richard tried the door, which was usually left on the latch. But it was locked.

'She's out,' he said. 'Bother! We've come all this way for nothing! What a waste!'

They went round to the back, but there was nobody in the garden. They saw a note pinned on the back door. 'One brown loaf, please.'

'Yes – she's out working somewhere,' said Sally. 'Well – never mind – we had a lovely walk.'

'I could have been doing my jigsaw,' said Richard, kicking a stone along crossly. 'Now we'll have to come all this way again and ask Mrs Ronaldson.'

'Cheer up, Richard!' said Sally. 'Maybe there was *some* reason why we came out on a useless errand to-day!'

'Don't be silly,' said Richard. 'I tell you, it was just a waste of time!'

They went back through the woods – and suddenly Sally clutched Richard by the arm. 'Look – oh, do look – a red squirrel! Isn't he lovely?'

The little red squirrel bounded up a tree-trunk, and looked at them with bright, dark eyes. And then something terrible happened. A boy's head popped up behind a bush, his arm went back, and a stone whizzed through the air

'LOOK – A RED SQUIRREL!'

SALLY RAN TO THE SQUIRREL.

straight at the little squirrel! It struck it on the head, and the little thing half-fell from the tree. Before it could recover itself, another stone came through the air and hit it on one of its back legs.

The squirrel tried to scamper along a branch, but it couldn't use its leg. It fell to the ground and lay there, struggling to get along.

Sally screamed. She ran straight to the squirrel. Richard ran straight to the boy.

99

'Oh, you horrid boy! What do you mean by throwing stones at a little red squirrel? You've hurt it – it did you no harm! You hateful, cruel boy!'

The boy laughed. 'Good shot, aren't I? Like to see me throw a stone at that blackbird?'

Richard had been told not to fight, but something boiled up inside him and he flew at the boy as if he meant to knock him down. The boy fended him off. He was much bigger than Richard.

'Go on, baby! You can't hurt me!' he said scornfully.

'Do you know what you are? You're the kind of boy who grows up into the sort of man who attacks the weak and the old!' shouted Richard, quite beside himself. 'My father's a policeman, and he's always telling us how cruel men start as cruel boys!'

When the boy heard that Richard's father was a policeman he disappeared at once. Richard went to Sally. She was crying over the little squirrel.

'Its poor eye, Richard! Look where the stone hit it. It'll be blind. And its leg is broken.'

'We'll take it home to Mother,' said Richard. 'She'll know what to do.'

So they took the poor little thing home, wrapped in Sally's scarf. It lay still, hurt and frightened, trembling all over its little furry body. It looked up at Sally with its one eye, and the little girl couldn't stop crying.

'It looked so sweet and happy, bounding up

THEY TOOK THE POOR LITTLE THING HOME.

the tree,' she said. 'Hateful boy! How could he be so cruel?'

Mother was sad when she saw the little squirrel. She felt its broken leg, and then very carefully she set the bones together, and tied a little splint to them.

'Its leg will heal, I think,' she said. 'But I'm afraid it will lose its eye. Poor little mite!'

The children kept the squirrel in a big box in the playroom. It was very good and very tame.

It ate the food the children brought, and watched them out of its one good eye. It loved Sally best of all.

'Dear little One-Eye,' said Sally, stroking the thick red-brown fur. 'How could anyone want to hurt a pretty little thing like you?'

The squirrel's leg mended. It could use it again, though it seemed rather stiff at first. The children were delighted when it scampered over the room. At first it didn't try to leap and bound, but soon it was frisking about gaily.

THE SQUIRREL'S LEG MENDED.

'You'd hardly know its leg had been hurt,' said Mother, delighted. 'But it will always be blind in one eye. One day the squirrel will leave you, Sally and Richard – but you mustn't mind. You can't keep a wild thing for long. It needs to go back to the home it knows.'

Little One-Eye did go back one morning. He chattered gaily first as if he were telling the children all about it, and thanking them for their love and care. Then he took a flying leap out of the window and was gone.

He didn't come back again. Sally was quite sad about it, but Mother soon cheered her up. 'Even if little One-Eye doesn't come to you, you can go and visit *him*! He will always know you and welcome you.'

'Well, let's go to the woods then,' said Sally. 'We'll go nutting! We'll take baskets, and bring you back lots of nuts, Mother!'

So off they went, Sally and Richard together. They came to the wood and searched the hazel trees for nuts. But there were hardly any – other children had been there first!

And then little One-Eye came bounding up! He leapt on to Sally's shoulder, and then on to Richard's. He was as pleased to see them as they were to see him! He chattered away in his funny little squirrel voice, and then bounded down to the ground in front of them.

'Let's see where he goes,' said Sally. 'Perhaps he will take us to his own special tree, where he has his hole.'

So they followed him. He took them to a

'LET'S SEE WHERE HE GOES,' SAID SALLY.

secret nut-copse where the hazel trees were laden with big nuts, ripe and brown! Some hung on the trees, some lay fallen on the ground. What a store of them!

'Goodness! Look at these nuts!' cried Richard, in surprise. 'One-Eye, you brought us here specially to get them, didn't you? You're a wonder!'

They filled their baskets, whilst One-Eye ran off with one or two nuts and carefully tucked them into holes in trees, so that he might hoard some for a winter day. In between his hunting and hiding, he was up to all sorts of tricks. He jumped into the children's baskets, leapt to their shoulders, frisked between their legs, and showed them quite clearly that they were his friends and he was theirs.

'We must go home,' said Richard at last. 'Our baskets are full.'

One-Eye came with them a little way, and then disappeared. As they walked out of the wood the children met two boys who stared in envy at their nuts. One of them was the boy who had thrown the stones at the squirrel.

'Where did you get all those nuts?' he called. 'I can't find more than two or three.'

But Sally and Richard wouldn't even answer!

'WHERE DID YOU GET ALL THOSE NUTS?' HE CALLED.

What, talk to that horrid, cruel boy? Not they!
He didn't deserve any nuts at all!

Little One-Eye is still in the woods. If you see
him, be kind to him, and he'll come bounding to
you. Wasn't it a good thing that Sally and
Richard went through the woods that autumn
day?

Quick! WHAT SHALL WE DO?

O
N the bookcase in the children's playroom there was a round glass bowl full of water. In it swam a goldfish, round and round and round.

The toys used to climb up and watch it each night. 'Why do you open and shut your mouth like that?' asked the bear. 'Are you drinking water all the time? You must be very thirsty.'

'Of course he's not drinking his water,' said the golly. 'Why, he would soon empty his bowl if he drank all the time!'

'Goldfish, do you like being in your little bowl?' asked the big doll, leaning over.

The goldfish swam to the top and stuck his big mouth out of the water. 'No. This bowl is too small,' he said. 'And I've no nice green weed, and not even a water snail to talk to. I'm bored.'

The toys were sorry for him. They went to

107

talk to him as often as they could. And then one night a dreadful thing happened.

The kitchen cat came stalking quietly in on her velvety paws. The toys fled to the toy cupboard. The cat stood inside the room, watching for any movement, her long tail swishing to and fro.

She suddenly caught sight of the bowl up on the bookcase, and she leapt lightly up to it. She sat by it, watching the big goldfish swimming round and round.

She put her paw into the water. The goldfish was full of alarm. He wriggled away, and the cat

THE CAT SPRANG DOWN.

108

pawed at him again. She stood up and put both paws in the water, trying to catch the frightened fish.

Well, you can guess what happened. The bowl suddenly slid to the edge of the bookcase and toppled over. The cat sprang down, frightened, and ran out of the door. The bowl struck the floor and broke in half. All the water came out and spread over the floor in a big shallow puddle.

The poor goldfish lay struggling on the floor. He couldn't breathe, because he had no water. The toys heard him flapping his tail on the floor and peeped out.

'Quick! What shall we do?' cried the golly, running out. 'The bowl's broken, the water's spilt – and the poor goldfish will soon be dead.'

'Oh, QUICK! What shall we do?' cried everyone.

'Water, water!' gasped the poor struggling goldfish. 'Take me to water.'

But there was no water in the playroom, not even a vase of flowers with water in it. The golly ran to the little garage of the dolls' house and flung open the doors. There was no car there, but there was a small doll's pram. The golly wheeled it out quickly. He shouted to the teddy bear.

'Help me to lift the goldfish into this. We'll wheel him to the pond in the garden. Quick!'

The bear, the golly, and the big doll lifted the heavy goldfish into the doll's pram. Then the golly wheeled it out of the door, down the

THE LIFTED THE HEAVY GOLDFISH INTO THE DOLL'S
PRAM.

passage, and out through the open kitchen door
into the garden.

They came to the pond. There was no movement at all from the poor goldfish now. 'He's
dead, I'm afraid,' said the bear. 'We weren't
quick enough.'

'Tip him in,' said the golly, and they tipped
him in. They watched him in the moonlight,
slithering down to the bottom of the pond and
then coming up again.

110

'His fins are moving! He's opening his mouth – he's shutting it!' cried the bear. 'He's alive. Look, he's swimming again!'

So he was. He swam slowly round the pond, marvelling at everything. What a place! Why, look at the lovely green weeds that he could wriggle in and out and round about, look at the watersnails he could talk to, look at the mud at the bottom that he could nuzzle his nose into! Wonderful!

The toys called down anxiously: 'Goldfish! We're so sorry about the accident. We did the

'I'VE NEVER BEEN SO HAPPY IN MY LIFE,' SAID THE
GOLDFISH.

111

best for you that we could. Are you very lost and unhappy?'

'Me?' said the goldfish, swimming right up to the top. 'I've never been so happy in my life. It was a WONDERFUL accident. This is a glorious place. I'm going to be very, very happy here.'

The toys were pleased. They went back to the playroom. 'Well, we did the best thing we could think of as quickly as we could,' said the golly. 'And it happened to be just right. Don't let's tell anyone where the goldfish is, in case they take him out of his lovely pond and put him into a new glass bowl.'

So they didn't say a word, not even to the cat. Everyone was most astonished next morning to find the bowl broken and no sign of the goldfish. It seemed very, very mysterious indeed.

He's still in the pond, but he's much bigger and fatter now. I'll show him to you if ever you come to my house.

THE DAY OF THE PARTY

SHEILA was so excited. She had been asked to Maureen's party on the eighteenth of January.

'Maureen has such lovely parties,' she told her mother. 'She says there is to be a conjurer this time. Oh, I do hope there is!'

'Now, you sit down and write a nice letter accepting the invitation,' said Mummy.

'Oh – can't you do it for me?' said Sheila.

'Certainly not – don't be so lazy!' said Mummy. 'Fancy expecting other people to do *your* jobs! You should be doing things for *me*, as well as doing your own little jobs.'

'Why don't you give her some duties to do?' said Daddy, putting down the newspaper he was reading. 'She doesn't even make her bed!'

'Well, I will,' said Mummy. 'I think she *has* been getting lazy lately.'

Sheila went red. Yes, she was rather lazy –
and she was careless, too. 'I'll do any jobs you
want me to,' she said to her mother. 'It's the
New Year now and I'm turning over a new leaf.
You tell me the jobs I must do, Mummy.'

Mummy looked pleased. 'Well,' she said,
'you certainly could make your bed each morning – but *properly*, mind – no pulling up the bed
clothes and that's all! And you might water my
plants for me every other day.'

'And she could pull each day's date off the
calendar by my desk,' said Daddy.

'Yes, I'll do that too,' said Sheila, thinking
that it would be rather fun to tear off each day as
it went by and see a new date appear each
morning. 'I like tear-off calendars. I'll make my
bed and water Mummy's plants and tear off
your calendar each day, Daddy.'

'Good girl,' said Daddy.

Well, Sheila kept her word. She made her bed
beautifully. She remembered Mummy's plants.
She tore off the days on Daddy's calendar.

'The eighteenth is coming nearer and nearer,'
she told Mummy. 'That's the day of the party!
It's the tenth now. Only seven and a bit more
days.'

The next morning Sheila got up late. 'Bother!
I can't stop to make my bed properly!' she said.
'I'll just pull up the clothes and hope Mummy
won't notice.'

But Mummy did notice, of course, and she
was cross. The next day Sheila forgot to water
the plants, and she didn't remember the third

114

SHE MADE HER BED BEAUTIFULLY.

day either. So two of them began to droop and die.

Mummy felt the earth in the pots. 'Oh, dear! It's as dry as can be!' she said. 'Sheila, you have forgotten to water my plants. It's too bad of you.'

'And who has forgotten to tear off my calendar?' said Daddy, looking at it. 'It says it's the twelfth, but it's the thirteenth.'

Sheila went sulkily over to the calendar and tore off yesterday's date. Then she went, still sulkily, to get the little watering-can for Mummy's plants.

'SHEILA! DON'T LOOK LIKE THAT!' SAID DADDY

'Sheila! Don't look like that!' said Daddy sharply. 'You took on the jobs, didn't you? Well, whatever jobs we take on, we have got to do as well as possible. Otherwise we are cheating.

'I'm sorry,' said Sheila, suddenly seeing that it *was* rather like cheating, if you didn't keep your word.

The next day she did well, but the day after that she slipped again and forgot everything! Mummy and Daddy didn't say anything, because Granny had suddenly fallen ill and they

116

were too worried to notice if Sheila was keeping her word or not. So she didn't bother about her jobs the next day either.

But on the following day she was so sorry because Mummy and Daddy looked terribly worried about Granny that she pulled herself together, made her bed properly, and watered all Mummy's plants. She didn't think about the calendar till after dinner.

Mummy had gone round to see Granny. Daddy was out at his office. There was nobody to remind Sheila about the calendar. But she suddenly caught sight of it and remembered.

'Gracious! I've forgotten that too. It says the fourteenth! I haven't torn it off for – let me see – three days!'

She went to the calendar and tore off a handful of dates at once. She thought she had torn off three – but in her haste she had torn off four. She threw the bits of paper into the waste-basket.

'There! That's done too. Now I've done all my jobs. What shall I do now? I know! I'll write a little note to Granny. She'll like that.'

So Sheila sat down at Daddy's desk and began to write her address at the top. Now the date. What *was* the date? She looked at the calendar. Oh, yes – the eighteenth!

She was just writing down 'January 18th' when she thought of something.

'The eighteenth! Why – that's the date of Maureen's party! It's *this afternoon*! Oh, my goodness me, what am I going to do?'

SHEILA SAT DOWN AT DADDY'S DESK

Sheila sat staring at the calendar. The day of the party – and Mummy was out – and her party dress wasn't ironed – and she didn't know where her best socks were – and, oh dear, Mummy had sent her best shoes to be mended!

'I shan't be able to go!' wept Sheila. 'And I did so want to. Oh, how *mean* of Mummy to forget! She doesn't love me a bit if she can forget the party. She knows how much I wanted to go.'

Sheila dried her eyes. She got up and went to

118

her bedroom. Yes, there was her party frock hanging on the peg, crumpled and un-ironed. Well, she would go in a crumpled frock! Better to go looking untidy than not at all. She pulled on her party frock. She looked for a party ribbon for her hair, but there were only her school ones there. Her party shoes were not in the cupboard. They couldn't have come back from the mender's. Her best socks were in Mummy's work-basket, with a big hole in one heel. Mummy hadn't even mended them for the party.

Sheila began to cry again as she dragged on the holey socks and put on her ordinary shoes. Now, where was her little cloak? Mummy had said she would put a new lining in, because the other was torn.

Oh, dear! The cloak was there – but there was no lining in at all. Mummy had taken it out, but hadn't put a new one in.

'It's too bad, it is really,' said Sheila, feeling very angry and upset. 'Mummy's forgotten simply *every*thing. It's not like her to forget and be careless.'

She sat and thought for a minute. 'Perhaps Mummy is punishing *me* for being forgetful and careless. I've been awful the last few days – haven't done any of my jobs properly. Oh, how mean of Mummy to punish me like that. I suppose she thought I wouldn't be able to go to the party! Well, I *shall* go! I'll go in a crumpled frock, old shoes, holey socks, and a cloak without a lining. Yes, I will!'

SHEILA BEGAN TO CRY AGAIN.

She went to the front door, her face all
tear-stained. Never mind – she was going to the
party, she was, she was!

She opened the front door – and, dear me,
there was Mummy coming up the path, looking
very cheerful, and carrying quite a lot of parcels.

'Granny's better!' she cried, and then she
stared at Sheila in surprise. 'Why – what are you
all dressed up for like that?'

'Because I'm going to the party,' said Sheila,

in a cross, sulky voice. 'You forgot about my party things! You didn't mend my socks, or line my cloak. You didn't iron my frock. And my party shoes are being mended, so I have to go in these old ones. You're horrid! But I mean to go to the party all the same, so there!'

Mummy took firm hold of Sheila's arm and led her indoors. 'Now, what is all this?' she said. 'How dare you talk to me like that? Do you

MUMMY COMING UP THE PATH, LOOKING VERY CHEERFUL.

MUMMY TOOK FIRM HOLD OF SHEILA'S ARM AND LED HER INDOORS.

want me to spank you? Because that's just what I feel like doing.'

Sheila burst into tears again and pulled herself away from her mother. 'You don't love me!' she said. 'You know how much I was looking forward to the party, and you haven't done a single thing about it. You meant me not to go, I expect.'

'I really don't know what you are talking about,' said Mummy, looking very stern. 'The party is not till to-morrow. It's on the eighteenth, as you very well know.'

'Well, it's the eighteenth *to-day*!' sobbed Sheila. 'Look at the calendar.'

Mummy looked. Then she gave a little laugh. 'Oh yes – it certainly shows the eighteenth, Sheila – but I'm afraid that's just a bit of your usual carelessness. You have torn off too many days. It's only the seventeenth to-day.'

And so it was, of course. Sheila picked up the newspaper, and there was the date – Thursday, January 17th!

She went very red indeed. Mummy looked at her with a serious face. She began to undo the parcels she had brought.

'Look,' she said, 'I knew your party was to-morrow – so I called at the mender's to fetch your best shoes. And here they are. And here is some beautiful blue lining I bought to-day for your cloak. And look, here is some new ribbon for your hair. And I have even bought you a new pair of socks to match your dress. But *you*, Sheila, met me with unkind words and sulky looks. Your silly mistake was due to your own carelessness in pulling off too many days at once – and that wouldn't have happened if you had done your job properly and taken one single sheet off each day. I am thoroughly ashamed of you.'

Sheila didn't know what to say. She had never felt so ashamed and sorry in her life. To think

SHEILA HAD NEVER FELT SO ASHAMED AND SORRY IN HER LIFE.

that she had thought all these horrid things about her mother – and all the time Mummy had been lovingly buying her things for the party.

'Don't be ashamed of me,' she cried. 'Let me be ashamed of myself and make up to you for everything. I'll never forgive myself – never. You're the best mother in the world, and I'm the horridest child.'

'Well, you certainly are very horrid some-times,' said Mummy, kissing her. 'But I'm always hoping you'll be better some day! Now you take off that frock and let me iron it. And whilst I'm doing that, you can lay the tea.'

Lay the tea? Good gracious, Sheila would do *any*thing – *any*thing to show Mummy what she thought of her, and to show her how sorry she was for her unkind words and silliness.

And she hadn't missed the party after all! Everything was all right again – if only she could make Mummy not ashamed of her any more.

Well, what would you do if you were Sheila – turn over a new leaf – or not? She did exactly what you would do – so now you know!

THE END

Books by **Enid Blyton** for young readers

The Boy Who Turned into an Engine	95p	☐
The Book of Naughty Children	95p	☐
A Second Book of Naughty Children	95p	☐
Ten-Minute Tales	75p	☐
Fifteen-Minute Tales	85p	☐
Twenty-Minute Tales	85p	☐
More Twenty-Minute Tales	95p	☐
The Land of Far-Beyond	95p	☐
Billy-Bob Tales	75p	☐
Tales of Betsy May	75p	☐
Eight O'Clock Tales	75p	☐
The Yellow Story Book	95p	☐
The Red Story Book	95p	☐
The Blue Story Book	95p	☐
The Green Story Book	85p	☐
Tricky the Goblin	75p	☐
The Adventurers of Binkle and Flip	75p	☐
Mr Pink-Whistle's Party	85p	☐
Merry Mr Meddle	50p	☐
Mr Meddle's Mischief	95p	☐
Don't Be Silly Mr Twiddle	95p	☐
Adventurers of the Wishing Chair	85p	☐
More Adventures of the Wishing Chair	95p	☐
Rag Tag and Bobtail	75p	☐
Tales from the Bible	£1.25	☐
Children's Life of Christ	£1.25	☐
Bedtime Stories and Prayers	85p	☐

All these books are available at your local bookshop or newsagent, or can be ordered direct from the publisher.

To order direct from the publisher just tick the titles you want and fill in the form below.

Name_____

Address _____

_____

Send to:
Dragon Cash Sales
PO Box 11, Falmouth, Cornwall TR10 9EN.

Please enclose remittance to the value of the cover price plus:

UK 45p for the first book, 20p for the second book plus 14p per copy for each additional book ordered to a maximum charge of £1.63.

BFPO and Eire 45p for the first book, 20p for the second book plus 14p per copy for the next 7 books, thereafter 8p per book.

Overseas 75p for the first book and 21p for each additional book.